One Day Raw Food Challenge

Experience Eating Raw Food for One Day
and *Feel* the Difference it Makes in Your Life!
With Wendy P. Thueson | "Raw Chef Wendy"

HAWAII WAY PUBLISHING
4118 West Harold Ct., Visalia, CA 93291
www.HAWAIIWAYPUBLISHING.com

HAWAII Way logo and name/acronym (Health and Wealth and Inspired Ideas) are registered and trademarked by HAWAII Way Publishing.
Copyright © *2016 Wendy P. Thueson*
The right of *Wendy P.Thueson* to be identified as the author of the work has been asserted by her in accordance with the Copyright, Designs and Patents Act 1988
All rights reserved.

No part of this publication may be reproduced, distributed or transmitted in any form or by any means, including photocopying, recording or other electronic or mechanical methods without the prior and express written permission of the author or publisher, except in the case of brief quotations embodied in critical reviews and certain other noncommercial uses permitted by copyright law.

HAWAII Way Author/Speakers Agency can send authors to your live event. For more information or to book an event contact HAWAII Way Publishing at:
HAWAIIWaypublishing@gmail.com, or 559-972-4168
Printed in the United States of America
ISBN-13: 978-1-945384-06-6
ISBN-10: 1-945384-06-6
Copyright © Raw Chef Wendy, LLC 2013, Eagle Mountain, UT, USA

First published in Utah by Wendy P. Thueson, Raw Chef Wendy, LLC in March of 2013. The second edition was published in April 2016 by Wendy P. Thueson for Amazon.com
Author may be contacted at rawchefwendy@gmail.com
Photography by Heather Walker Studios and Raw Chef Wendy, LLC

Disclaimer:
The techniques and advice described in this book are a representation of the author's opinions based on her personal experience and are not in any way intended to diagnose, treat, prescribe, or cure any condition you may be experiencing. The author does not in any way claim responsibility for any liability, loss or risk, personal or otherwise, which is incurred as a result of using any of the techniques, recipes or recommendations suggested herein. If in any doubt, or if medical advice is required, please contact the appropriate health practitioner or professional.

CONTENTS

Welcome from the Author	1
What You Can Expect	2-3
60 Benefits to Eating Raw	4
Affirmations for a Raw Food Lifestyle	5
Please Read This First	6-7
Your 1 Day Raw Food Challenge	8
Menu Break-Down	9
Instructions for this Menu	10
Shopping List	11-12
Check-In for Day 1	13
Recipe Section	14-22
Breakfast	15-16
Lunch	17-18
Dinner	19-20
Dessert	21-22
Check-In for Day 2	23
Compare & Share	24
Congratulations & More Information	25-29
Resources	30-32

WELCOME

Hi, I am Wendy P. Thueson, owner of Raw Chef Wendy, LLC, and I am so excited to be sharing this 1 Day Raw Food Challenge with you.

Whether you want to add more uncooked, raw fruits and vegetables to your current meals or want to dive in and see what this is all about for you, this one-day guide will help you understand step-by-step how to get started and have success.

Raw foods are fruits, vegetables, and sprouted nuts and seeds that are uncooked and alive when we eat them. The seeds of these various foods are actually able to be planted in the soil and watered. Together with sunshine, they will grow into plants because they are not killed by heat from cooking. Keeping the heat around 105 F. is the temperature I like to recommend, but the enzymes do not start to die until close to 125 F. I use my finger as a 'thermometer' to help me know when to take the food off the heat source. Sometimes we just need a little warm food, so this helps me remember, "If it's too hot for your finger, it's too hot for your body and the enzymes."

Cooked foods, on the other hand, are heated at high temperatures, which kills the life-giving enzymes and makes a person tired and run-down. The high heats also create chemicals, such as acrylamide, that are carcinogenic (cancer-causing) and can harm the body in other ways. The key to remember here is that raw foods make a person feel alive. Cooked foods make a person feel tired and run-down over time and they actually move us toward death faster.

My desire is to help you learn how to add more of these amazing raw foods to what you currently eat, in hopes that you will want to change your habits over time and reach for the delicious, live, vibrant colored raw foods instead of the dead, toxic, cooked and processed foods.

I can tell you from my own experience of overcoming chronic fatigue of 28 years, Grave's disease, brain fog, and many more symptoms, that my life has improved dramatically as I have cleansed, nourished and strengthened my body by eating a high amount of raw plant foods. We really are what we eat. Take this challenge and feel the difference for yourself.

WHAT YOU CAN EXPECT

Just 24 hours of eating raw is not a very long time, but it is surprising to most people how just one day is enough to see some results. Imagine five days or one month eating this way! Don't worry, we'll get there together. I remember learning all I could about raw food and thinking it was so complicated. I went to culinary school so this should be easy, right? Wrong. Many of the ingredients I had never heard of before like Maca, Lucuma, Irish Moss, Cacao, Gogi berries, and the list went on. But I quickly learned these were considered "super foods" and were not necessary to use in the beginning if I didn't want to deal with them.

My first attempts at making a simple Green Smoothie were frustrating. I like to make things up as I go along but this technique didn't work in this new world of food preparation. I didn't know what I was looking for with flavors and textures because I was using unfamiliar ingredients. So I stuck to simple recipes and kept trying until I found some I liked. Then I studied to learn how to use these and other unique ingredients and I experimented with them. Over time I have become quite proficient with raw food and the ingredients and can play around in the kitchen again. The key to my success is – Never give up!

Everybody is different, so your experience and results will range according to the following factors:
- What you are eating currently
- How you are feeling as a result of years of eating what you eat
- How much you eat (overeating or not eating enough will lessen the effects)
- Your current beliefs about your body and the possibility that you can succeed
- How closely you stick to the plan and not "cheat"

This is not a diet fad; it is a lifestyle that can be very beneficial to anyone who tries it for extended periods of time. I have also learned in my experience with raw food that because I have been dealing with addictive behaviors toward sugar and carbohydrates, I have needed to take things one day at a time. Trying to see the bigger picture of the rest of my life has been too big and discouraging for me. I felt overwhelmed and fell back into my old behaviors. So, look at this as one day to see how you feel and then we'll go from there.

BENEFITS

On the next page I have listed 60 benefits I have personally experienced by eating a diet high in raw foods. Please read through each one and see how many of them you identify with. My hope is that this will motivate you to keep going. Use this and the affirmation sheet that follows to help you get through any negative emotions or experiences you may have during the day.

TRACKING

I have also included tracking pages for you to track your progress. Please fill these out and be as honest and thorough as you can be. This is not for anyone else to read, unless you want to share the information. It is intended for you to refer to and keep as a journal while you go through this raw food journey.

JOURNAL

A journal is very important to record how you are doing each day. I highly encourage you to keep a journal to track your progress with health, emotions, relationships, spirituality and all aspects of your life. You will be able to have evidence to show someone who does not believe you. It is also a powerful reminder of where you have been and how far you have come. In the many years I have been eating this way, I have had a difficult time remembering all of the symptoms I once experienced because they are no longer a part of my life. I go back to my journals and records of these experiences from time to time and can't believe how far I've come.

EXTRA HELP

If you are struggling and need extra help, please refer to the Resource section or contact me through my website at www.rawchefwendy.com. When changing the way you eat, you may experience a variety of symptoms or changes with medications, etc. Please contact your health care professional for help with these and other serious issues.

CLEANSING

Introducing more raw foods can be very cleansing to the body so it is good to stay close to a restroom for the first day or two. Consider doing this over a weekend so you can rest as well.

60 BENEFITS TO EATING RAW

The following is a list of the many benefits Wendy has experienced going raw. Imagine what can happen to you!

More ENERGY
More STAMINA
More ALERT
My body feels CLEAN inside and out
No more DIGESTIVE ISSUES
Neck & Back PAIN GONE
No more GAS & BLOATING
Clear SKIN
Improved LIBIDO
Less SLEEP needed
I EAT less
No more INFLAMMATION
No more CONSTIPATION
Balanced BODY TEMPERATURE
No more DEPRESSION
Improved EYESIGHT
No more ANXIETY
I lost 10 pounds
I am at the IDEAL WEIGHT for my body
I love the TEXTURES of the food
I love PREPARING food again
I feel HAPPIER
I am more MOTIVATED
I'm over my sugar ADDICTION
I've learned not to care what others think
I do this to TAKE CARE of myself
I want to HELP PEOPLE
I am an INSPIRATION to my family
I feel like I have a PURPOSE
I wake up REFRESHED every day
My TEETH don't hurt anymore
I don't get DEPRESSED like I used to
No more STUTTERING
I love the COLORS of the food
I'm not HUNGRY all of the time
I love the TASTE of the food
More ENERGY
More STAMINA
More ALERT
My body feels CLEAN inside and out

I am an INSPIRATION to others
I feel more SPIRITUALLY in tune
No more PAIN
I have PURPOSE
I want to keep my SURROUNDINGS clean and organized
I have energy to EXERCISE
I am more IN-TUNE with my body
I have lost the desire for SWEET foods
I don't need the SALTY foods either
I have LEARNED MORE ABOUT MYSELF

I LOVE who I AM
I have more LOVE for OTHERS
My EYES don't hurt anymore
I have COMPASSION for people in my situation
My SEASONAL ALLERGIES are gone
I wake up EXCITED for each new day
I am PASSIONATE about sharing this MESSAGE
I LOVE what I DO
I love CREATING new dishes
I like DISCOVERING new INGREDIENTS
I am not afraid to be SOCIAL anymore
I am meeting LIKE-MINDED, AMAZING people!
There is LESS TRASH
Most of the 'trash' can be COMPOSTED

I feel SATISFIED after a meal and ENERGETIC
The STUFFED, TIRED feeling after a meal is GONE
No more MUCOUS in the morning
I am an INSPIRATION to others
I feel more SPIRITUALLY in tune
No more PAIN
I have PURPOSE

AFFIRMATIONS for a Raw Food Lifestyle

Affirmations are statements that you can say to yourself that are positive and encouraging. They are in the present tense because our minds believe that what we say is actually happening now. There is enough negative self-talk in our minds to keep us from succeeding at anything. That is why these affirmations are so powerful. They literally change your self-defeating talk into self-loving talk that has the power to help you conquer the world!

These affirmations are to help you through challenging times. Changing over to a new way of eating can be a little rough at times and these affirmations will help support your efforts as you make small or big changes each day.

Say them in a whisper and then yell them out and make big gestures with your hands to show power and self-love. Doing this in extremes helps them sink into the mind and body. Just watch, you will start to BELIEVE them as you do this every day and a transformation will have to take place.

Choose three or more of these affirmations to focus on -- or make up your own -- to say every day to yourself.

I am AMAZING!
I LOVE and RESPECT my body!
I LOVE eating Raw Foods!
I LOVE the way Raw Foods make me feel!
I feel INSPIRED to live my best life!
I know who I am and I LOVE ME!
Preparing and eating Raw Foods is EASY!
I feel CLEAN inside and out!
I am an AMAZING example of health and vitality to all those around me!
My body LOVES when I eat clean, raw foods!
I feel INSPIRED to make the necessary changes to be
my IDEAL self!

PLEASE READ THIS FIRST

On the following pages you will find a Menu Plan, a Shopping List, Recipes, and Tracking Sheets for one full day of eating the Raw Food way.

If you happen to come up against any of the following challenges…

- ❖ Food allergies to one or more of the ingredients
- ❖ Not liking an ingredient or two
- ❖ Not being able to find or purchase one or more of the ingredients
- ❖ Not liking the sound of a recipe in the menu

… please do not worry! In most recipes, one or more of the ingredients can be substituted with a different ingredient that is similar to it. For example, if you don't like spinach, use kale, Spring lettuce mix, or any other dark, leafy lettuce you can find. If you do not like zucchini or cannot find it in a particular time of year, use a different kind of squash for the vegetable noodles or even carrots, beets, or other vegetables you like. Most recipes are easily adapted and may even taste better with your favorite ingredients. There is no right or wrong here; experiment and have fun in the kitchen and create your own original raw food dishes.

If a particular recipe does not appeal to you, then find a different recipe that does and go with that. There is no need to feel stuck by having to use ONLY the recipes provided here. There are other wonderful recipes on my website at www.rawchefwendy.com that may look more appealing to you. Choose one or more and go for it! Create your own menu plan, shopping list, and recipes if you wish, because you call the shots!

If for some reason you feel hungry, eat some snacks in between meals of fruit, vegetables or sprouted nuts and seeds.

SPROUTING NUTS & SEEDS

Nuts and seeds can be soaked 30 minutes to overnight to get the enzyme inhibitors off of them and to get them to start sprouting. Refrigerate after soaking and rinsing or dry thoroughly before using in trail mix and other recipes, snacks, etc.

Your body is in a fasting and cleansing state during the night. It is very helpful to continue this cleansing process in the morning when you wake up.

I always start my morning with 1-2 green apples and at least one glass of distilled water. Distilled water helps the body clean out the inorganic minerals that have accumulated in various organs and part of the body but it does not touch the organic materials. The Green Smoothie helps this cleansing process also.

During the warmer months I often drink a full blender of smoothie throughout the morning. This gives me plenty of nutrition and added hydration and allows the contents to come to room temperature. After my daily workout of alternating running and yoga or lifting weights every other day, I have a protein shake within 30 minutes of my workout to help build the muscles.

Just starting out, schedule at least a 30 minute walk every day and finish with a plant-based protein shake or snack that does not contain sugar, soy, wheat, or whey, and a large glass of pure water. Then continue with the remainder of the menu and add nourishing snacks as needed.

You can do this! Get started now.

~ Wendy P. Thueson | "Raw Chef Wendy"

One Day Raw Food Challenge

MENU BREAK-DOWN

First Thing in the Morning

- ✓ 1 or 2 Granny Smith apples or other variety of apple or piece of fruit
- ✓ Water – at least one to two glasses to rehydrate the body

Breakfast

- ✓ Green Smoothie or Protein Shake (good after exercise)

Lunch

- ✓ Large Fruit & Nut Salad with Vinaigrette Dressing

Dinner

- ✓ Vegetable Pasta with Fresh Marinara Sauce

Dessert

- ✓ Frosted Brownie Bites

Snacks

- ✓ For on-the-go snacks, prepare a Ziplock® bag of cut up vegetables, a bag of grapes, or a bag of sprouted nuts.

    See the note on page 6 SPROUTING NUTS AND SEEDS to learn how to sprout nuts and seeds.

Drinks

- ✓ Water (distilled is great when cleansing and for herbal teas, and just to drink throughout the day; if you don't have distilled water or cannot get it easily, you can look for a counter distiller on www.amazon.com or online, or just drink the purest water you can find)
- ✓ Fresh juices (organic and not pasteurized are the best)
- ✓ More smoothies if desired

INSTRUCTIONS FOR THIS MENU

Decide what day you will be doing this One Day Raw Food Challenge and mark it on the **calendar**. A weekend may work best for your first time as you may need to be home during cleansing.

1-2 days before:
- Go shopping for ingredients listed on pages 11-12.

The day before:

- Gather all of your equipment: A basic blender will do for this menu although a BlendTec® or Vitamix® high-speed blender would be ideal. Be sure you have a cutting board, sharp knife, a spiralizer if possible, and any other equipment stated in the recipes.

- The brownies may be made ahead of time and put in the refrigerator with a lid on top to keep them fresh.

- You may also decide to make ahead the marinara and spiralize or cut the zucchini, but DO NOT mix them together. Put them in separate containers.

The day of:
- Complete questions on page 13, "Check-in for Day 1," as soon as you wake up. This will only take a few minutes and is very important to record how you are feeling.

The next day:
- Follow each recipe as outlined and continue throughout the day.
- Complete questions on page 23, "Check-in for Day 2," as soon as you wake up. If you want to continue eating this way, print out another copy of this page so you can continue recording how you are feeling.
- Compare how you feel now to how you felt upon waking the first day on page 24, "Gathering Evidence." Is there any difference? What specifically did you notice? Record your observations.
- Repeat this Challenge as often as you'd like.

SHOPPING LIST

Purchasing organic, wherever possible, is preferable for health reasons and because they taste much better too. If money is an issue, do not let that put you off. You will still find it beneficial to eat this way with conventional fruits and vegetables. Remember too that you will be eating much less than you are used to eating, so the cost of groceries will most likely go down or be about the same.

FRUIT
- ☐ Bananas
- ☐ ½ cup dried cranberries, sweetened with fruit juice (I purchase mine in the bulk section of the health food store)
- ☐ 3 Granny Smith apples
- ☐ ½ cup fresh raspberries
- ☐ 2 cups mixed fruit such as melon, peaches, mango, pineapple, strawberries, etc.
- ☐ 2 cups frozen or fresh peaches (for Peach Cobbler Shake on page 16)
- ☐ 1 Mandarin orange
- ☐ 2 cups Medjool dates, pitted

VEGETABLES
- ☐ 3-5 large handfuls of fresh organic spinach, Spring mix, kale, or other dark leafy greens or a mixture of any of these
- ☐ 4 large tomatoes, diced
- ☐ 2-3 Tablespoons onion, diced
- ☐ ½ clove garlic, minced
- ☐ Any vegetable to make into noodles (zucchini, yellow squash, carrots, beets, etc.), 1 per person

NON-DAIRY ITEMS
- ☐ 2 cups fresh almond milk

NUTS
- ☐ ½ cup pecans, soaked for 1 hour or overnight and rinsed
- ☐ 2 cups walnuts, soaked overnight and drained

MISCELLANEOUS ITEMS
- ☐ 2 Tablespoons lemon juice
- ☐ 2 Tablespoons red wine vinegar
- ☐ ¼ cup olive oil

SPICES
- ☐ Sea salt
- ☐ Cinnamon
- ☐ 1 teaspoon Kirkland's® Organic No-Salt Seasoning (I get mine at Costco)
- ☐ 1 teaspoon Italian spice blend
- ☐ 1 cup cacao powder, dark chocolate cocoa (not Dutch processed) or carob powder
- ☐ 2 teaspoons pure vanilla

OPTIONAL SUPPLEMENTATION
- ☐ 1 scoop green shake powder mix (optional)
- ☐ ½-1 scoop protein shake mix (optional)
- ☐ Organic Essential Oils
  See resource section on page 30 for my recommendations

CHECK-IN FOR DAY 1:

Please complete this FIRST THING in the morning upon waking!

On a scale of 1-10, with 10 being the best you can feel, how do you feel upon waking this morning? (Circle one)   1 2 3 4 5 6 7 8 9 10

Look in the mirror. How does your face look?
1. Blotchy and red
2. Puffy
3. Eyes swollen with dark rings around them
4. Other _____

Stick out your tongue. How pink is it?
1. It is not pink. It is white!
2. Quite pink with some white
3. A nice, clean pink with no white
4. Other _____

What kind of mood are you in?
1. Grumpy. I want to go back to bed.
2. Tired. I want to go back to bed.
3. Okay.
4. Happy. I felt like I had a good night's sleep.
5. Energetic! I'm ready to take on the day!
6. Other _____

Please write down any other comments about things you notice upon waking this morning:

_____
_____
_____
_____
_____
_____
_____
_____

One Day Raw Food Challenge

RECIPE SECTION

BREAKFAST

Here are three different smoothie recipes you can choose from. They are all delicious and very nutritious. Have them for breakfast, after a workout, or for a snack. You can do all three!

GREEN SMOOTHIE
Yield: 2 cups

Leafy greens are the key to success on raw food. They are full of protein, fiber and many nutrients that clean and rebuild your body in amazing ways. One or two glasses a day or a blender full, like I often do, will help your body feel new and vibrant. Green is your new favorite color and the taste is divine!

Equipment: Blender, preferably a high-speed blender
Ingredients:
1 large, ripe banana
2 cups mixed fruit such as melon, peaches, mango, pineapple, strawberries, etc. (This can be a frozen mix without added sugar or fresh fruit you have on hand. Berries may also be added but will change the color.)
1 cup purified water
3-5 large handfuls of fresh organic spinach, Spring mix, kale or other dark leafy greens. (You may also do a mixture of greens for more nutrition.)

Instructions:
1. Blend all ingredients in high-speed blender.
2. If you prefer your smoothie to be a little more liquid, add water until desired thickness is achieved.
3. When you are ready, pour yourself a tall glass of Green Smoothie and drink with chewing motions to activate the saliva for better digestion. Enjoy and be sure to share with your loved ones.

> ### *Raw Chef Wendy's Tip:*
>
> *I love to make a blender full of Green Smoothie to drink throughout the morning.*
>
> *There are some days, however, when there is some left over. I like to either refrigerate it for the next snack or meal, or spread it out on a Teflex® sheet and put it in my Excalibur® dehydrator to dry for fruit leather.*

PROTEIN SHAKE
Yield: 1 ½ cups

    Sometimes you just need a little more plant-based protein in your life. I have a wonderful company I use to get mine (see Resources on page 30). Blend it up with the remaining ingredients and enjoy.

Equipment: Blender, a regular one is fine
Ingredients:
8 ounces pure water
1 scoop protein powder mix*
½ - 1 scoop sprouted green powder mix*
1 large banana (you may also add other fruit like berries, peaches, strawberries, etc.)

Instructions:
1. Put ingredients into the blender in order given. Blend until smooth.
2. Add water if too thick or if adding more fruit, until desired consistency is achieved. Pour into a glass and drink up!

PEACH COBBLER PROTEIN SHAKE
Yield: 4 cups

    I love peach cobbler, but the gluten and sugar in it don't love me back. So I made this recipe to enjoy whenever I think of eating peach cobbler because it is so much better for me. My kids love it too and ask me to make it for snacks and dessert.

Equipment: Blender
Ingredients:
16 ounces or 2 cups of fresh almond milk or pure water
1 scoop Protein Shake powder mix
1 large banana
1 cup frozen or fresh peaches (if using fresh, add 1 cup ice)
Dash of cinnamon

Instructions:
1. Blend all ingredients in order listed above until
2. Enjoy!

LUNCH

This is usually the largest meal of the day for me. I take a large dinner plate and fill it with greens and then add other fruits and nuts, vegetables, avocado and a dressing. Lettuce is a neutral to add either fruits or vegetables to, but do not do both. For digestive reasons they do not mix well.

WENDY'S FAVORITE SALAD

Yield: 1 serving

Equipment: Knife & cutting board, blender
Ingredients:
½ cup pecans, soaked for 1 hour or overnight and rinsed
2-3 large handfuls of lettuce (green leaf, Spring mix, spinach, or a combination of lettuces you like)
1 Granny Smith apple, diced
½ cup dried cranberries sweetened with fruit juice (can be found in the bulk section of the health food store)
*pomegranate seeds can be substituted for the cranberries when in season
1 Mandarin orange, cut into wedges
Balsamic Vinaigrette [recipe on page 18]

Instructions:
1. On a large dinner plate, spread out the lettuce and add the remaining ingredients on top.
2. Serve with vinaigrette dressing below.

BALSAMIC VINAIGRETTE

Yield: 1 cup
Equipment: Bowl and whisk
Ingredients:
1/4 cup balsamic vinegar
2 teaspoons maple syrup
1/2 teaspoon sea salt
1 Tablespoon garlic, minced
1/2 teaspoon fresh ground pepper
1/2 cup extra virgin olive oil
1/4 cup water

Instructions:
1. Whisk together all ingredients in a bowl.
2. Serve over salad.
   * This will keep in the refrigerator for several weeks.

DINNER

I love pasta, but since I became gluten intolerant I am not able to have the traditional pasta anymore. Thank goodness for vegetables and a Spiralizer®, which can be found at Amazon.com. It makes great noodles you can use as a base with any fresh sauce for a delicious meal.

VEGETABLE PASTA
Yield: 1 serving
Equipment: Spiralizer or knife and cutting board, food processor
Ingredients: Any vegetable to make into noodles (zucchini, yellow squash, carrots, beets, etc.), 1 per person

Marinara Sauce:
4 large tomatoes, diced
¼ cup sun-dried tomatoes in olive oil
1 Medjool date, pitted
2-3 Tablespoons onion, diced
½ clove garlic, minced
1 teaspoon Kirkland's® Organic No-Salt Seasoning
1 teaspoon Italian spice blend

Instructions for Vegetable Noodles:
1. Wash and cut vegetables into 3-inch chunks length-wise, leaving the skin on if organic.
2. Put the rectangle chunk into the spiralizer and follow manufacturer instructions to make spaghetti noodles.
3. Put on a dinner plate in the amount you want and set aside.

Instructions for Marinara Sauce:
1. Chop tomatoes and onions in a food processor or by hand with a knife, until slightly chunky or smooth if you prefer.
2. Add remaining spices and pulse or mix in a bowl until blended.

~ Instructions continued on next page ~

3. At this point you may warm this up slightly in a skillet with about 1 tablespoon olive oil and put the noodles in to warm, using the finger as a guide.
4. **Remember:** if it is too hot for your finger, it is too hot for your body.
5. You may put the noodles back on the plate and do the same with the marinara; then top the noodles with the sauce, or you may mix them both together and warm. Mixing them together may cause them to become a bit mushy. This may also be eaten cold. Other sauces such as pesto may be used over the noodles.

DESSERT

This is my favorite recipe for Raw Brownies. I got it from a dear friend who I used to be in a Raw Food club together with. We would get together once a month and bring various raw food dishes to taste and share recipes. These brownies were the hit one month and continue to be the star of the show when I bring them to any party or teach them at my classes. They are rich, chocolaty and so easy to make!

MY FAVORITE BROWNIES
Yield: 1 pan
Ingredients:
2 cups Medjool dates, pitted
2 cups walnuts, soaked overnight and drained
½ cup cacao powder

Instructions:
1. In a food processor, blend up the dates until smooth and they form a paste. A ball will form and spin around the food processor bowl. Take out the dates and put into a bowl.
2. Chop up the walnuts in the food processor until ground fine.
3. Put the date paste back in the food processor with the nuts and add the cacao powder. Blend until smooth.
4. Put into a glass 8" X 8" brownie pan and press into the bottom and sides of the pan. You do not need to grease the pan.
5. Refrigerate and make the frosting. [recipe below]

FROSTING:
1/2 – 2/3 cups raw honey or Grade B maple syrup
1/2 cup cacao powder
Dash salt
1/4 teaspoon cinnamon
2 teaspoons vanilla
4 Tablespoons coconut oil

For a Mint Tasting Frosting Add:
2-3 drops mint essential oil (optional)
 *See Resource section on page 30 for more information on recommended oils.

Instructions:
1. Combine all ingredients in the order listed in food processor and blend until smooth, about 1 minute.
2. Spread on top of brownies and refrigerate until firm.
3. Cut into small pieces and serve.

Raw Chef Wendy's TIP:

These brownies are rich, so I make them into small brownie bites and place them on a plate or tray to serve.

They are great any time of the day for a snack or dessert.

CHECK-IN FOR DAY 2:

Please complete this FIRST THING in the morning upon waking!

On a scale of 1-10, with 10 being the best you can feel, how do you feel upon waking this morning? (Circle one)   1   2   3   4   5   6   7   8   9   10

Look in the mirror. How does your face look?
1. Blotchy and red
2. Puffy
3. Eyes swollen with dark rings around them
4. Other _____

Stick out your tongue. How pink is it?
1. It is not pink. It is white!
2. Quite pink with some white
3. A nice, clean pink with no white
4. Other _____

What kind of mood are you in?
1. Grumpy. I want to go back to bed.
2. Tired. I want to go back to bed.
3. Okay.
4. Happy. I felt like I had a good night's sleep.
5. Energetic! I'm ready to take on the day!
6. Other _____

Please write down any other comments about things you notice upon waking this morning:

_____
_____
_____
_____
_____
_____
_____
_____
_____
_____

COMPARE & SHARE

Compare the two Check-In sheets. What did you notice that was different **physically** from Day 1 to Day 2?

_____
_____
_____
_____

What did you notice that was different **emotionally** from Day 1 to Day 2?

_____
_____
_____
_____

What did you notice that was different **mentally** from Day 1 to Day 2?

_____
_____
_____
_____

What did you notice that was different about your **appearance** when you looked in the mirror from Day 1 to Day 2?

_____
_____
_____
_____

You just gathered **facts** to prove whether raw food actually works for you or not. Even the slightest differences can be noticed when you are paying attention.

CONGRATULATIONS!

You have successfully completed the

One Day Raw Food Challenge

More AMAZING raw food awaits you with Wendy's delicious recipes.

Continue your journey of health and high energy in the following pages.

The next step is to attend classes with

Learn how to prepare even more delicious Raw Food!
It's time to invest in your health for prevention and to enjoy a richer lifestyle full of energy and fun!

THERE IS MORE AVAILABLE TO SUPPORT YOU

More Books

Online Programs

Private Chef Courses

Little Chef Summer Camp

Online Market

Monthly Newsletters

Magazine Articles

Television Appearances

Conferences

Retreats

& Much More!

Visit www.rawchefwendy.com and get involved.

Wendy's RAWinspiring Recipe Series begins with her Reasonably Raw recipe book.

Make the comfort foods you are used to like pizza, tacos, soups, sandwiches, and much more by 'healthifying' them with Wendy's tips.

- ❖ Reduce the amount of meat, dairy and eggs you use
- ❖ Increase the amount of vegetables and fruits in each dish
- ❖ Decrease the temperature to preserve the enzymes
- ❖ Learn when to add spices to dishes for medicinal enhancement
- ❖ Get amazing tips for organizing your kitchen and supporting your new lifestyle!
- ❖ And SO much more!

Visit www.rawchefwendy.com for more information and to order. This book is also on www.amazon.com.

Wendy's RAWinspiring Recipe Series continues with her Beautifully Raw recipe book.

Increase the amount of raw food you eat for greater health, energy and stamina by creating these amazing dishes from Wendy's book. Recipes like:

- ❖ Pizza Rolls
- ❖ Rainbow Salad
- ❖ Chocolate Pudding
- ❖ Spring Rolls with Thai Ginger Sauce
- ❖ Coconut Macaroons
- ❖ And SO much more!

All recipes are plant-based and are perfect for people with food allergies. They do not contain animal products, wheat, gluten, soy, dairy, processed sugars, etc.

Visit www.rawchefwendy.com for more information and to order.
This book is also on www.amazon.com.

RESOURCES

*PURIUM®

When I first went raw, I was a sugar addict and was attempting to get off of processed foods, so I naturally replaced the sugar with fruit. The problem was, I also had a yeast overgrowth or Candida. This was very uncomfortable for me and difficult to control. If you do not know what this is or the symptoms associated with it, they can be as follows:

For Men: Athletes foot, fungus in fingernails and toenails, jock itch, etc.
For Women: fungus in fingernails and toenails, vaginal itching and discharge anywhere from thin yellow color to a thick cottage cheese appearance.

These and other symptoms can occur when the body is out of pH balance. This has to do with the amount of acid or alkalinity we have in our system. We need a more alkaline than acid environment: 7.2 on the pH scale is about neutral. The more acidic we are, the more prone to sickness and disease we become. A cold or flu are a bit more acidic and cancer is very acidic. This has a great deal to do with what we eat and it can be difficult to achieve a consistent balance with food alone.

I also live in a seasonal climate with harsh winters. We get our food mostly trucked in from warmer climates. We are able to grow gardens but the growing season is pretty short. The food that is trucked in is picked green and does not have the added nutrients and benefits of tree-ripened fruit. I have tried to eat 100% raw and in this climate and region of Utah, I am unable to sustain this kind of lifestyle all year 'round.

That is why I highly recommend the Purium® products. They are great for supplementation for nutrition that we are lacking and to help keep the pH balanced. Because of the pesticides, hormones, lack of nutrients in the soil and toxins in the air and water, we need some help to maintain balance.

Here are a few facts: They are a certified organic facility that manufactures products for over 200 different companies. David Sandoval is a cofounder of the Purium® company and is a world-renowned Phytochemist. The company has been around for over 23 years. Their ingredients are pure and my body recognizes the high energy and frequency in them.

I have been approached by many different companies to try their products and even create a raw food line for them. I did for one that went global but integrity was not intact, so I left. I have been searching over 7 years to find the right supplementation for me and I have finally found Purium® which exceeds my high expectations. I no longer am plagued with symptoms of candida, inflammation, chronic fatigue, debilitating neck and back pain or any other of the many symptoms I've carried with me over the years. I also finally feel an underlying sense of nutritional balance that I was not able to obtain solely with raw food.

There are over 50 products which are organic, gluten-free, dairy-free, soy-free, whey-free and egg-free. The L.O.V.E.® Shake is full of plant-based protein from organic fermented rice protein and contains 20 grams of protein in 4 scoops. I also love the Power Shake with its amazing profile of organic greens. I blend these with a banana in my shakes in the morning (see recipe section on page 14) and drink an entire blender full.

I do not recommend products with whey protein isolate or other dairy products for many reasons because this is a very highly processed product at high heats and is not good for the body. Choose plant-based ingredients and look on the labels for ingredients that are derived from plant sources, not synthetics.

To learn more about the products and the company visit: mypuriumgift.com
Use the gift card code *rawchefwendy* **for $50 off your first order.**

Essential Oils I Recommend

** There are many essential oils companies out there, but the quality varies greatly. The #1 word you need to see on the label is **ORGANIC**. If it doesn't say "Certified Organic" then it isn't. The essential oils are the life blood of the plant and they are a very concentrated form - up to 100 times! The body utilizes the essential oils immediately and it uptakes all of the extras like pesticides, toxins and sewage sludge with it, if it is NOT "Certified Organic" or "Wild Crafted" (Wild Crafted means they are not farmed, but taken from the wild where the plants have not been sprayed and they are in their natural environment).

    I recommend the essential oils from **Purify® Skin Therapy**. They are USDA Certified Organic and Wild Crafted and are sourced by Holly Draper, the only certified Medical Aroma Therapist in the State of Utah as of 2016. She is highly educated on the safety, use and efficacy of essential oils and after using essential oils from upwards of 6 different companies, these are the only ones I will use. Smell them for yourself and feel how quickly they absorb and work on your body.

To learn more about them please use this link:
https://www.purifyskintherapy.com/?tracking=286

*Wendy does receive a small amount of affiliate income from using this link which helps further spread her message. Thank you for your support.

Sourced by a Certified Medical Aromatherapist

Certified Organic ● Wildcrafted ● 100% Pure ● GC Tested

Wendy P. Thueson is also known as Raw Chef Wendy. She is a certified Chef, Master Herbalist and Raw Food Coach. She is passionate about the healing power of plants and sharing her message of hope with others because of her life changing experience regaining her health in 2009. She suffered from chronic fatigue for 28 years, debilitating neck and back pain, brain fog, stuttering, Grave's disease, and hypoglycemia to name a few.

Wendy began eating a high amount of raw foods and using herbs medicinally. As a result, she is now symptom, pain and medication free. She educates all ages through hands-on classes, speaking at various events, and has been featured on television, radio and in magazines. She has authored several books and online programs to help others learn how to eat and live happier lives. You may find her at www.rawchefwendy.com

"Your One Day Raw Challenge was inspiring and motivating. I loved what I learned in the information you shared. I also love what you have on your website and can't wait to get started learning more with your online program."

~Linda

"Wendy, I really enjoy your classes and the food you make is so delicious! Thank you for sharing your recipes and knowledge with us."

~ Denise

www.ingramcontent.com/pod-product-compliance
Lightning Source LLC
Chambersburg PA
CBHW042000080526
44588CB00021B/2817